The Planted Seed

The Immutable Laws of Sowing and Reaping

Juanita Bynum

Pneuma Life
PUBLISHING

The Planted Seed

Unless otherwise indicated, all scriptural quotations are from *The Holy Bible–King James Version.*

The Planted Seed
ISBN 1-56229-122-X

Pneuma Life Publishing
Post Office Box 885
Lanham, MD 20703-0885
(301)577-4052

Visit our webpage at http://www.pneumalife.com

Contents

to fully comprehend. Pastor Austin laid his hand on my little head and, with Holy Ghost boldness, began to decree the word of the Lord. When he removed his hand, I experienced what felt like a heat wave go completely through my body. At that moment–that very instant–God planted a seed in my spirit!

As I grew older, my life began to become quite chaotic. My mother would always say to me, "Juanita, I don't care what Satan is doing right now in your life. I know what *God* said, and I'm going to stand on the promises of God!"

It's life changing when you have a praying mother who says with powerful conviction, "I am standing on the promises of God!" Her words would ring out with such authority that you could sense Satan being halted in his tracks.

At times, when I was stumbling and being beaten up by the enemy, I could still hear a small voice down on the inside of me saying, "I am the Lord your God. I have called you by My Name, and I desire to use you in a great and mighty way."

God, You've Got The Wrong Juanita!

There were seasons in my life when the enemy would seriously challenge my calling. It was during those seasons when I felt like Gideon–when the angel of the Lord appeared to him, and he thought the angel had the wrong address.

I have said on several occasions, "God, you must have me mixed up with another girl named Juanita. There are several of us in the earth, you know. I just know I am not the right one, especially after all that has happened to me!"

As time went on, however, I began to see God's hand in my life. I watched Him turn my life upside down and inside out. He began to bless me, both spiritually and naturally, in ways you would not believe.

I became more and more excited about God's Word. As I began to soar in God, I knew there was no turning back! My heart and my entire being began to say "Yes!" to God's will. Hence, I completely surrendered my will to Him.

The Manifestations of the Seed

I began to move out on the things God had shown me. The things He had spoken in the past began to manifest themselves before my eyes. Doors were being opened, and God was moving by His Spirit! Sick bodies were being healed, and old and young alike were turning their lives over to Jesus as never before in my ministry. To all those things I said, "To God be the glory!"

ing God to do a work for her as she goes. This way, you won't embarrass yourself."

At this point, I could not get into fear because I was in God's presence. The Lord began to say, "I am the Lord that healeth! Speak the Word, and command this woman's leg to bend in the Name of Jesus!"

I grabbed her leg and commanded it to bend in obedience to His voice. Then I began to praise God. At first, nothing happened.

Suddenly, the young woman began to walk down the aisle. When she reached the end, she turned around, bent her knee and began to dance in the Holy Spirit! To God be the glory!

While heading back to the hotel, I began to meditate and praise God for such an awesome move of His Spirit. I rejoiced for the healing that sister had received.

As I reflected on what God had done, I imagined how she must have been feeling. It had to be wonderful for her to once again, after five years, have the ability to sit in a chair and bend both her knees. I also gave thanks for the two souls who came to Jesus, and I meditated on how wonderful they must have felt to be free from the clutches of the enemy.

While I was rehearsing in my mind the victories that had taken place that evening, the minister who was driving said, "Sister, God is going to use you in an even greater way before this meeting is over."

When he spoke those words, something hit my spirit! I quickly said "good night" to the other saints in the car, hurried to my hotel room, double locked the doors and said, "God, would you please tell me what's going on?" I waited for His reply, and He said nothing–zilch! I did not hear one, single word from Him!

What Happens When You Say, "Yes Lord!"

The next morning, I was awakened by a telephone call from the crusade leader. He informed me that the Christian radio station in Greensboro had heard that I was a young woman being used of God, and they wanted to do a live interview with me.

That afternoon, I went to the radio station to do the interview. I sat there thinking, "Lord, things are really moving against my intellect. Lord, I don't know what is happening. I don't know anything about going on radio or physical miracles. Lord, I just don't know what I'm doing!"

The Lord responded very gently, saying, "Juanita, that's because you're not the one who is doing the work–I Am!"

A scary feeling came over me. I thought to myself, "Is this what takes place when a person says 'yes' to

The B

The hostess infor
they would be
young evangelist wh
With my mind blank,
Lord", I boldly steppe

In that moment, God
told them that I was in
ment. I went on to say
iting that city. I proph
bring strong deliveran

Something broke in
and when the Holy Spi
fifteen minutes had ela
ence of God that paraly

taries and other station employees had begun to cry in acknowledgment of the Spirit of God.

They were so moved, they attended the meeting that night. The conviction was so strong, they were convinced that I was sent by God to that city and felt an urgency in their spirit to make the divine appointment.

The whole city seemingly came alive. The phone lines at the station were immediately jammed with people requesting prayer. Something had changed.

Open Your Mouth, and I Will Fill It

When I arrived at the service the second night, lo and behold, the building which comfortably held three-hundred fifty people was filled! Chairs lined the hall and everywhere a body could be, one was there.

I tried to look poised, as if I had it all together, but all I kept thinking was, "Lord, if you would just tell me what's going to happen next, I would feel much better. How about just a little bit of feedback, huh?"

I approached the podium and stood there for a moment. I didn't have a prepared message. I didn't know what I was going to say because God had not given me a message.

As I stood there, the Holy Spirit spoke to me and said, "I am the speaker, not you. Put your trust in Me. Open your mouth, and I will fill it."

I opened my mouth and asked, "How many people came tonight looking for a fresh drink from the Holy Spirit?"

Immediately, as if someone had thrown a bomb, the power of the Holy Spirit fell inside that building. I really believe that if someone had taken a picture of me at that moment, my eyes would have been bulging out of my head like the character, Buckwheat, in the old television sitcom "The Little Rascals".

The place erupted in the Spirit! People came hurriedly to the altar to be saved while others were filled with the Holy Spirit. There was a mighty move of God that night!

Once again, following the service, God began to deal with me. He let me know that in this last-day move, the Holy Spirit will not need just an intellectual or analytical mind to work through; He will use vessels who are willing to lose themselves totally in Him and yield to what He wants to say and do.

The Power Is In His Presence

The next night, as I ended the message, you could feel the presence of God hovering in that place. I began to pray in the Spirit to get further direction from the Lord.

After a minute or two, a word of knowledge came up in my spirit. I spoke it out saying, "The lady with the brace on your leg–Jesus wants to heal you." A woman wearing a plastic brace came forward, and I prayed for her. She went back to her seat rejoicing because the pain had left.

Again, the Holy Spirit spoke through me and said, "There is another lady here with a brace on. Please come out into the aisle."

The first woman's leg was in the healing process after spiritual surgery. However, when I asked for the second woman, a much older woman wearing a leg brace stepped forward.

When she stepped out I asked, "Lord, You're trying to embarrass me, right?" He responded, "Relax in Me and follow My leading."

The woman came to the front, sat down, and took the leg brace off. I stood over her and began to pray in the Spirit.

The Lord let me know that when you pray in the Spirit, it ushers you straight into His presence–and where He is, there is no fear, doubt or worry. When in His presence, you stand in complete assurance that every word He has ever spoken will come to pass!

There was a spiritual drive inside of me that went beyond just belief; it was an absolute confidence in my "knower". I had no doubt in my mind at all. Actually, before she even got up, I saw her in the Spirit, already walking.

I quickly pulled her to her feet, and she began to walk and give God the praise! She had not walked without that brace for more than 35 years!

At that point, I stopped questioning God about what He was doing and began to move with the flow of the Holy Spirit. I have learned that when you simply yield to the will of God, He will begin to show Himself mighty–*to* you, *in* you, and even more so, *through* you!

The Origin

You must understand that all of the events that took place in the crusade didn't just fall out of the clear, blue sky. Nothing in this world suddenly jumps into existence. Everything has an origin. Everything has its beginning–though hardly recognizable–at the point of manifestation.

First, there must be a process by which a seed of some sort is planted–whether by word or deed, spiritual or natural, good or bad.

The planting of seeds is the method God has ordained for all things to come into existence. That is how, as stated in the book of Isaiah, *He declares the end from the beginning.* God puts the ending of a thing in the seed, and when He is ready to begin that particular thing, He plants the seed.

do we protect that seed from the clutches of Satan once it has been planted?

The first thing we must do is change our perception of seeds to God's perception of seeds.

Bruising the Head of the Enemy

Did you know that the first prophetic word spoken in the Bible concerning defeating Satan mentions a Seed?

Jesus, Himself, was a Seed sown into the world by the Father in order to destroy Satan. Notice when the Father wanted to destroy the power of the enemy, He released a Seed–His Son, Jesus Christ! This shows us the power of seed planting; just as Jesus did whatever He saw the Father do, we should do likewise. Remember, the servant is not above his Master.

Even though a seed may seem small and insignificant, it is powerful, in the hands of God, in bruising the head of the enemy and destroying his power. This is what you are protecting until its time of fruition.

God is the same yesterday, today and forever, and we, His children, are made in His image. So, when we want to defeat the enemy in our lives, we do it by releasing a seed. God then anoints that seed and destroys the work of the enemy.

There is simply no way Satan can defeat a giver. This is why he fights us so hard in our giving. The only way he can win is if you hold onto your seed. Givers are releasing seeds that bruise his head.

Now he that ministereth seed to the sower both minister bread for your food, and multiply your seed sown, and increase the fruits of your righteousness. 2 Corinthians 9:10

Now, let's look at the Living Bible translation:

For God, who gives seed to the farmer to plant, and later on, good crops to harvest and eat, will give you more and more seed to plant and will make it grow so that you can give away more and more fruit from your harvest.

This Scripture refers to giving as a seed. God not only multiplies our seed, but He uses it to crush the authority of the enemy.

In the Scriptures, the head represents authority. The head of Christ is God, the head of the man is Christ, and the head of the woman is the man (1 Corinthians 11:3). When we speak of bruising the head of the enemy, it means attacking and destroying his authority.

Whatever authority the enemy is exercising against a believer, in any area, it can be broken with a seed.

Think about it. The enemy has exercised authority against our finances, marriages, bodies, children and churches. The enemy has also exercised authority in our families for generations. Curses of poverty, lack, debt, promiscuity and destruction need to be broken in the lives of many.

The authority of the enemy in these areas needs to be bruised by the sowing of seeds into the Kingdom of God. To bruise means to crush, to injure, to hurt. It is taken from the Hebrew word "shuwph" meaning "to snap, overwhelm and break". Your giving overwhelms the enemy. Your seed breaks, bruises and crushes any authority he may be trying to exercise against you. Don't underestimate the power of your seed.

Following are several Scriptures that must take root in your spirit:

> He that observeth the wind shall not sow; and he that regardeth the clouds shall not reap. Ecclesiastes 11:4

> He that goeth forth and weepeth, bearing precious seed, shall doubtless come again with rejoicing, bringing his sheaves with him. Psalm 126:6

> Give, and it shall be given unto you; good measure, pressed down, and shaken together, and running over, shall men give into your bosom. For with the same measure that ye mete withal it shall be measured to you again. Luke 6:38

> Now he that ministereth seed to the sower both minister bread for your food, and multiply your seed sown, and increase the fruits of your righteousness. 2 Corinthians 9:10

There is that scattereth, and yet increaseth; and there is that withholdeth more than is meet, but it tendeth to poverty. Proverbs 11:24

To become a recipient of the manifestations of God flowing through you, there must be a sowing (planting) of God's Word in your spirit.

Sowing

The sower soweth the word. Mark 4:14

This is the first and most important step. It is important for you to realize that God cannot schedule your harvest until He has your seed. You can only sow what God's Word says to sow in order to reap the blessings of God. In other words, you can't use the methods of the world to get what God has for you. They will never work.

Everything you sow must line up with God's Word and His will for your life. It must be a spiritual transaction as well as a verbal affirmation, in accordance with the Word of God.

Why? Because if God's method for blessing us was based on how much money we earned or our savings, some of us would never drive new cars, live in fine homes, or wear nice clothes. If we were to reach out and try to obtain these things on our own, we would wind up frustrated and in over our heads in debt. Then, there goes our peace of mind and our physical health!

Sowing in the Spirit

In order to receive that which only the Spirit of God can bring into existence, the seed you plant [sow] must be done in the Spirit.

> For he that soweth to his flesh shall of the flesh reap corruption; but he that soweth to the Spirit shall of the Spirit reap life everlasting. Galatians 6:8

You must sow according to the Word of God. Looking back at the miracles that were wrought during the crusade in Greensboro, North Carolina, I realized that a spiritual seed was planted in the spirit within me. It was nourished and cultivated, and in the right season, it came to pass.

All of the blessings of God come through the principle of sowing first, and then reaping.

Success in your ministry, business or personal life does not just evolve; it is determined by the type of seeds you have sown within those areas. Your outcome or harvest will not and cannot exceed your input!

We need to understand that what we receive is not determined by the person that gives it to us. It is determined by our giving. What we give determines what we will receive.

Even your income is not determined by what people give you, but by how much you give. Your income solely depends on you. You determine your own income. It can increase or decrease according to the seed you sow.

The preacher's reward comes, not by the service that he or she does but by the seeds that they sow.

Whatever we receive as a return is determined only by what we give.

The Thief

And these are they by the way side, where the word is sown; but when they have heard, Satan cometh immediately, and taketh away the word that was sown in their hearts.

Mark 4:15

Satan comes immediately to steal that "word" out of your heart. Have you ever wondered why? First, it is a part of his character. The Bible tells in John 10:10, "The thief cometh not, but for to steal, and to kill, and to destroy..."

We must fully comprehend this characteristic concerning the devil. The ultimate reason he comes "immediately" to steal the word is because he knows that

God's Word has the power to take root and GROW immediately.

To clearly understand the creative operation of the Word of God, let's look at what took place during the creation of the world.

In the beginning God created the heaven and the earth. Genesis 1:1

Notice when God said, "Let there be light", there was light. And when God said, "Let the earth bring forth the living creature after its kind", they came into existence right then and there!

In the beginning was the Word, and the Word was with God, and the Word was God. The same was in the beginning with God. All things were made by him; and without him was not any thing made that was made. John 1:1-3

Since God is the Word, and the Word is God, and everything was made by His spoken Word, we must understand that every word of God–every promise of God–has the power to BE the moment it is spoken!

Why is this? Simply because every spoken word of God has the power to CREATE!

This is why Satan must come immediately to steal God's Word from our hearts. He knows that the moment it is properly received, it will immediately take root and manifest itself. So, whatever you do, don't allow Satan to steal that word from your heart. Remember the power of the tools given to you in bruising the head of the enemy. Stand firm on every Word of God!

The Importance of Roots

When we enter a flower garden, we immediately admire the beauty of the garden with our natural eye. We rarely take the time to stop and analyze the process by which it came into existence; we just enjoy what we see.

If we took the time to analyze this beautiful garden, we would realize that a plant not does have its inception on top of the ground. A seed must first be planted.

Therefore, what we see on the surface is only the result of that which was planted underground. In order to have a healthy plant, the following three elements are necessary: soil, seed, and in all cases, healthy roots.

The life of a plant is in its roots. If the roots aren't healthy, the tree is not healthy. If the roots are contaminated, if the roots are dead, the plant will not produce anything. This brings us to a very vital passage of Scripture:

> And these are they likewise which are sown on stony ground; who, when they have heard the word, immediately receive it with gladness; And have no root in themselves, and so endure but for a time: afterward, when affliction or persecution ariseth

Jesus (the Seed), wrapped in flesh, was pressured, persecuted and whipped until His flesh died. His flesh is symbolic of the outer shell of the seed. He came in the shell of human flesh. When His side was pierced, healing virtue spilled forth. When that outer man (outer shell) is broken, then your spirit is renewed.

This is the only way the life that is within the seed can spring forth: the outer shell must be pressured until it is broken–pressured, not moved or dug up!

Consequently, during those times when you begin to feel pressure from the enemy, you should be praising God for the "breaking process" of the outer shell rather than getting fearful and fretful. Be very careful–doubt will dig up your seed!

At this point, your seed should be so important to you that nothing is worth losing out on what God has for you. Right now, if you have already planted a seed, begin to release any unforgiveness or grudges you may be harboring against anyone. If you fail to do this immediately, you will impede the growth process of your seed. Don't allow offenses from others to stop your blessings from coming to pass.

Three Major Devices of the Enemy

And these are they which are sown among thorns; such as hear the word, And the cares of this world, and the deceitfulness of riches, and the lusts of other things entering in, choke the word, and it becometh unfruitful. Mark 4:18,19

I honestly believe it is at this point where most Christians totally lose out on their blessings. Notice that Jesus spoke of three major devices of the enemy (Satan) that will choke the roots of our seed:

1. Cares of this world,
2. Deceitfulness of riches,
3. Lust for other things.

Let me explain this to you in detail. Some of you never give money, time, or service to anyone or anything without first analyzing every facet of that to which you intend to give. Many Christians make excuses that sound something like this, "If I give $50.00 to my church, I'll have to live on a tighter budget the rest of the week."

This is a trick of the enemy!

Even a stockbroker is aware that he has to invest a larger amount in order to receive a larger return.

There are still other Christians who say,"If I stay at church past 9:00 p.m., I won't be as sharp on my job the next day", or "If I go and help out at the Saturday women's fellowship breakfast, it will totally ruin my Saturday!"

You can readily see that these people have become totally caught up with the cares of this world, thus completely hindering their walk of faith; when, in fact, everything we do within our Christian walk must be done in faith.

Romans 14:23 tells us, "...whatever is not of faith is sin!" 2 Corinthians 5:7 instructs us, "For we walk by faith, not by sight." Also, let us not forget Hebrews 11:6 which admonishes us, "without faith, it is impossible to please him [God]."

Anything you give to the work of the ministry must be given in faith. You must not become overly concerned about the way the world system operates. You must not become such a scrutinizer that you choke the very roots of the seed which you have planted!

It is God's will that you give because it is in giving that you receive.

Don't Sabotage Your Crop

If the enemy can't stop you from giving, he will turn around and try to make you sabotage that which you have already given.

Read what the apostle, Matthew, has to say about this:

Wherefore, if God so clothe the grass of the field, which to day is, and to morrow is cast into the oven, shall he not much more clothe you, 0 ye of little faith? Therefore take no thought, saying, What shall we eat? or, what shall we drink? or,

> Wherewithal shall we be clothed? (For after all these things do the Gentiles seek:) for your heavenly Father knoweth that ye have need of all these things. But seek ye first the kingdom of God, and his righteousness; and all these things shall be added unto you. Matthew 6:30-33

There you have it, straight from the mouth of Jesus! When you follow the principles of giving God's way, it has to come right back to you.

When operating within God's law of reciprocity, it is no longer necessary to seek after deceitful riches such as the lottery, horse racing or other aspects of gambling in order to become successful. Why should you gamble when you have obtained, through God's Word, a sure way to always win?

You don't have to lust for and covet that which belongs to your neighbor. Lust and covetousness are also tricks of the enemy (Satan). The dictionary states that lust is "an overmastering desire". It is not God's will for us to have overmastering, tormenting desires. It is His will, however, that we may be "...perfect and entire, wanting nothing" according to James 1:4.

Release Your Faith

Giving place to any of these temptations will result in choking the roots of your seed, thereby causing hindered growth.

Get rid of that old way of worldly thinking and begin to walk in Christian maturity. Release your faith and watch God work!

If you have already planted a seed, pause for a moment and think about the kind of seed you have planted and the soil you have planted it in. Begin to pray in the Spirit and clean your soil (your heart).

Make sure there is nothing in that soil–such as jealousy, malice, unforgiveness, envy, strife, discord or lust–which would hinder the growth process of your seed. Make sure there is nothing in that soil which would cause your seed to become malnourished.

Chapter 4

The Harvest of Your Seed

Now that you have cultivated your soil and properly nourished your seed, you are ready to receive what you have planted. This brings us to the third group of people mentioned in Mark 4:20:

> And these are they which are sown on good ground; such as hear the word, and receive it, and bring forth fruit, some thirty-fold, some sixty, and some an hundred.

These are the people who are experiencing the trauma of waiting. Many of you are saying, "Now that I have done all according to God's Word, where is the promise?"

My brothers and sisters, you are losing faith because you don't see any results. Thus, you conclude, erroneously, that God isn't working on your behalf.

Oh, my friends, take courage right now! Remember, Hebrews 10:35, where the Word admonishes us:

Do not cast away our confidence, for it has great recompense of reward. The Amplified Bible

The Living Bible interpretation says, "Do not let this happy trust in the Lord die away, no matter what happens. Remember your reward!"

For ye have need of patience, that, after ye have done the will of God, ye might receive the promise. Hebrews 10:36

God is working for you this very minute! Release yourself into the realm of the spirit and begin to look at this concept with your spiritual eyes, not your natural eyes.

God Is Not Limited

You can only see so far with your natural eyes. However, when you begin to see with your spiritual eyes, there are no limitations. Why? Because you are seeing through the eyes of God, Himself, and God is not limited!

The concept of the seed is much more powerful than you can imagine. The life of a tree is in its roots, and the strength of a tree is determined by the strength of its roots.

Let's look at the palm tree.

Did you know that the palm tree, a symbol of warm weather and the tropics, is able to return to its original state after a terrible storm? Why is this so? It is because of its roots. Regardless of what is happening on top, its roots are firm and full of life!

After the storm has passed and the sun is directly overhead, casting its warm rays, that palm tree remains beautiful because its source of life emanates from its roots.

As believers, our source of life emanates from the Word of God, sown and correctly applied in our lives. No matter what the adversity in our lives may be, understand and know that because our roots are firmly anchored in Jesus, what He has promised will surely come to pass.

Your job is to keep your heart right so the roots can remain firmly planted. One day, we are going to wake up to the fact that Satan stirs up storms to change our hearts because he cannot stop us. He applies external pressures which are geared at causing us to make a change on the inside of us.

Those who can focus and walk in the spirit will know the blessings of God.

While we look not at the things which are seen, but at the things which are not seen: for the things which are seen are temporal; but the things which are not seen are eternal.

2 Corinthians 4:18

How can Satan stop something that is eternal if it never begins or ends? He tempts us to abort it in our hearts while it's in transition from Heaven to earth.

God Wants Fruit That Remains

Two weeks had passed since God first spoke to me concerning writing this book. I asked Him when He wanted me to finish the book, but there was no response.

Finally, after three weeks had passed, He spoke to me again. I was lying down, but I was very restless that Sunday night. I tossed and turned so much that I finally got up and went into the kitchen with my Bible. It was 3:00 a.m.

When I opened the Bible and began to read, the Holy Spirit spoke to me and said, "Get your book and write." When I turned to the next blank page to begin to write, the Holy Spirit spoke so powerfully that at first I couldn't write anything. I just sat in His presence and listened.

There are times when you come into the raw presence of God, and no flesh can move. All you can do is bask in the Spirit.

He said to me, "Juanita, I desire to bless my people, but I also desire to bring forth out of them the kind of fruit that will remain."

Look at Abraham. God promised him a son. The right spiritual seed was planted, and he waited on God. Even when his wife, the closest person to him, laughed in unbelief, Abraham's faith in what God had promised was not shaken! This was the lineage of Isaac, the son of promise.

It is the ordained will of God that His people bring forth both spiritual and natural fruit.

> Ye have not chosen me, but I have chosen you, and ordained you, that ye should go and bring forth fruit, and that your fruit should remain: that whatsoever ye shall ask of the Father in my name, he may give it you. John 15:16

When God speaks a word of promise, His method of blessing you cannot be different from the process He has stated in His Word. Because He is the Word, it is impossible for Him to deviate from that which He has spoken. God is immutable!

It is essential that we come into the realization that the moment God speaks the Word, the intangible is brought into existence.

Examine the incident concerning the fig tree in Mark 11:12-14, 20.

When Jesus spoke to the fig tree, it died then and there. The moment He cursed it, its roots died, but the death of the tree wasn't immediately apparent; that is, big toe, until the man of God taught me how to take a deep breath, and jump in.

That reality hit me in my spirit like a ton of bricks! I received what the man of God said and took the plunge of faith. I began to give like crazy! I stopped looking at how much money I could afford to give and began to give what the Holy Spirit was telling me to give.

You may ask, "Did it hurt?" Yes, it did!

Pastor Boyd would say things like, "Now it's time to give. When I count to three, jump up and shout, 'Hallelujah!', because God loves a cheerful giver!"

The first few times, my "hallelujahs" were so faint, you would have to climb down my throat to hear them. Many times I went to the offering basket feeling like I had an active ulcer and had just drank an entire bottle of Texas hot sauce!

I literally gave until it hurt, but never begrudgingly. I began to give in the manner in which I wanted to receive.

Becoming Mature In Giving

Yes, obeying the voice of God in giving is a very difficult thing to do at first, but, after a while, you will begin to develop such a love for God that you will say, "Lord, what else can I do to please You?"

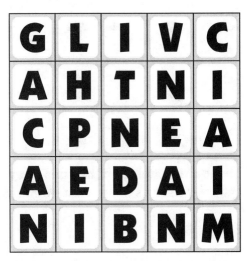

Find **four Asian countries** word-winding their way through the grid of letters.

Find a **single nine-letter word that uses every letter**
(one time) word-winding its way through the grid of letters.

Find a **single nine-letter word that uses every letter**
(one time) word-winding its way through the grid of letters.

Find **four common eight-letter words** word-winding
their way through the grid of letters **from top to bottom**.

_____

_____

_____

_____

Find **two seven-letter words** word-winding their way through the grid of letters—one **from left to right**, the other **from right to left**.

Find **two seven-letter words** word-winding their way through the grid of letters—one **from left to right**, the other **from right to left**.

Find **two seven-letter words** word-winding their way through the grid of letters—one **from left to right**, the other **from right to left**.

J	A	I	G	K
D	A	Y	T	E
T	P	N	A	I
H	A	I	T	L
Y	A	C	Y	V

Find **four countries** word-winding
their way through the grid of letters.

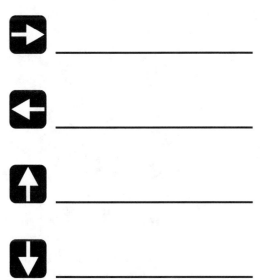

→ _____

← _____

↑ _____

↓ _____

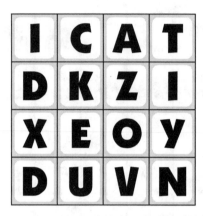

Find a **single ten-letter word that touches all four corners** word-winding its way through the grid of letters.

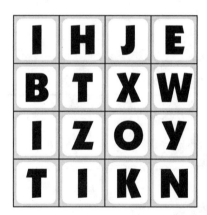

Find a **single ten-letter word that touches all four corners** word-winding its way through the grid of letters.

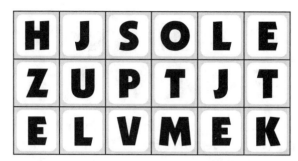

Find **two six-letter words** word-winding their way through the grid of letters—one **from left to right**, the other **from right to left**.

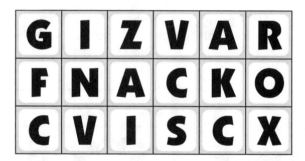

Find **two six-letter words** word-winding their way through the grid of letters—one **from left to right**, the other **from right to left**.

Find **two six-letter words** word-winding their way through the grid of letters—one **from left to right**, the other **from right to left**.

Find **two six-letter words** word-winding their way through the grid of letters—one **from left to right**, the other **from right to left**.

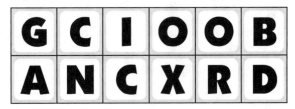

Find **two six-letter words** word-winding their way through the grid of letters—one **from left to right**, the other **from right to left**.

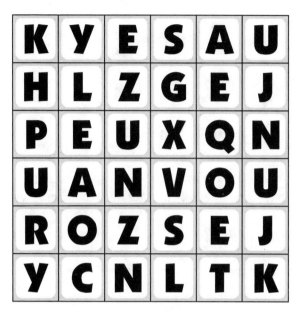

K	Y	E	S	A	U
H	L	Z	G	E	J
P	E	U	X	Q	N
U	A	N	V	O	U
R	O	Z	S	E	J
Y	C	N	L	T	K

Use the clues to help you find the **six-letter answers** word-winding their way through the grid of letters.

➡️ **Muppets creator** _____

⬅️ **Maker of the XJ8** _____

⬆️ **Pair, duo** _____

⬇️ **Follow-up film** _____

Find **two six-letter words** word-winding their way through the grid of letters—one **from left to right**, the other **from right to left**.

Find **two six-letter words** word-winding their way through the grid of letters—one **from left to right**, the other **from right to left**.

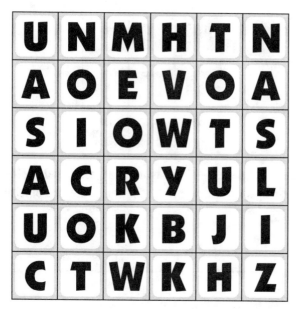

U	N	M	H	T	N
A	O	E	V	O	A
S	I	O	W	T	S
A	C	R	Y	U	L
U	O	K	B	J	I
C	T	W	K	H	Z

Use the clues to help you find the **six-letter answers** word-winding their way through the grid of letters.

➡ **Boeing competitor** _____

⬅ **Greek goddess** _____

⬆ **Paris** ____ _____

⬇ **Home to Red Square** _____

Find a **single nine-letter word that uses every letter** (one time) word-winding its way through the grid of letters.

_____

Find a **single nine-letter word that uses every letter** (one time) word-winding its way through the grid of letters.

_____

Answers